Elizabeth
BLACKWELL

WOMEN IN SCIENCE & TECHNOLOGY

BY ELAINE A. KULE

ILLUSTRATED BY ELENA BIA

New York Infm.

Rourke®

ROURKE'S
SCHOOL to HOME
CONNECTIONS
BEFORE AND DURING READING ACTIVITIES

Before Reading: *Building Background Knowledge and Vocabulary*

Building background knowledge can help children process new information and build upon what they already know. Before reading a book, it is important to tap into what children already know about the topic. This will help them develop their vocabulary and increase their reading comprehension.

Questions and Activities to Build Background Knowledge:

1. Look at the front cover of the book and read the title. What do you think this book will be about?
2. What do you already know about this topic?
3. Take a book walk and skim the pages. Look at the table of contents, photographs, captions, and bold words. Did these text features give you any information or predictions about what you will read in this book?

Vocabulary: *Vocabulary Is Key to Reading Comprehension*

Use the following directions to prompt a conversation about each word.

- Read the vocabulary words.
- What comes to mind when you see each word?
- What do you think each word means?

Vocabulary Words:
- *cleanliness*
- *courage*
- *equally*
- *practice*
- *recovered*
- *society*
- *surgeon*
- *wounded*

During Reading: *Reading for Meaning and Understanding*

To achieve deep comprehension of a book, children are encouraged to use close reading strategies. During reading, it is important to have children stop and make connections. These connections result in deeper analysis and understanding of a book.

 Close Reading a Text

During reading, have children stop and talk about the following:

- Any confusing parts
- Any unknown words
- Text to text, text to self, text to world connections
- The main idea in each chapter or heading

Encourage children to use context clues to determine the meaning of any unknown words. These strategies will help children learn to analyze the text more thoroughly as they read.

When you are finished reading this book, turn to the next-to-last page for **Text-Dependent Questions** and an **Extension Activity**.

TABLE OF CONTENTS

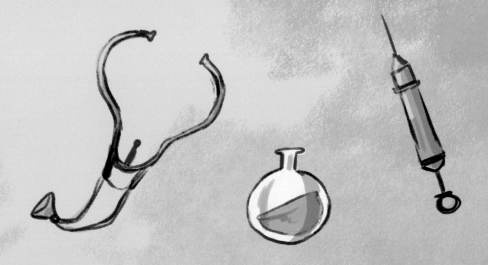

EARLY DAYS

Elizabeth Blackwell was born in 1821 in Bristol, England. She was the third of nine children. She was smart and rather shy.

Mr. and Mrs. Blackwell thought everyone should be treated **equally**. Their daughters and sons received the same education. The children had many books. Elizabeth loved reading them.

Working Against Slavery
The family believed that no one should own other people. They disliked how common slavery was in the United States. Elizabeth went to protest meetings as a teenager in New York.

Mr. Blackwell had a sugar factory. In 1828 a fire destroyed the building. The business never **recovered**. Mr. Blackwell moved the family to New York City in 1832. He opened another sugar plant. He later sold it. The Blackwells traveled to Ohio to start over. But many companies throughout the nation were doing poorly.

Mr. Blackwell died weeks later. The family was penniless. Elizabeth, then 17, started a school in their home. She, her mother, and two older sisters taught children. The school closed in 1843 when it stopped doing well. Elizabeth found other teaching jobs.

When Elizabeth was 24, a dying friend encouraged her to become a doctor. She said women might want a female treating them. But women doctors were unheard of then. Women could not even vote!

Elizabeth wanted things to change. "If the present arrangements of **society** will not admit of woman's free development, then society must be remodeled, and adapted to the great wants of all humanity," she once said. Elizabeth moved south to teach music at a women's college. She studied with a willing doctor in her free time. She also taught Sunday school to slaves. This was against the law at the time.

STRUGGLES AND SUCCESSES

Elizabeth met a well-known doctor. He sent a letter supporting her to a medical school in New York. But its professors did not want a female student. They also did not want to upset the doctor. They decided to accept Elizabeth if the entire class agreed. They were sure the young men would say no.

Several classmates thought the letter was a joke from students at another school. But most understood the reason behind their teachers' plan. They thought it was silly. They voted for Elizabeth. She happily entered Geneva Medical College in 1847.

Elizabeth's classmates teased and insulted her. But she did not react to them. Instead she worked hard. The students grew to respect her.

Good and Bad News
There were more female medical school students in the U.S. than males for the first time in 2017. But there are still fewer women teachers and leaders at medical schools.

One day a professor needed to teach the group about certain body parts. He asked Elizabeth to leave the room because he thought that she would be embarrassed. She promised to go if that was what the others wanted. Her classmates said Elizabeth should stay. She did!

Elizabeth earned the highest grades in the class. In 1849, she became the first woman to receive a medical degree in the United States. Elizabeth was thrilled! She hoped to be a **surgeon**.

Experience helping patients is another part of becoming a doctor. Elizabeth heard that hospitals in Paris, France, offered good training. She decided to spend a year there.

But Elizabeth developed an eye disease while working at a Paris hospital. She became sightless in one eye. Her dream of being a surgeon vanished.

Elizabeth moved to London, England, in 1850 to work at a hospital there. One day she met Florence Nightingale. Florence was a nurse who became famous for treating soldiers during wartime.

Elizabeth and Florence knew that **cleanliness** helps stop diseases. They taught people that hand washing keeps germs from spreading.

Elizabeth returned to New York City in 1851. She opened a medical **practice**. People were angry. They did not think women should be doctors. No one came to see her. A women's rights champion named Horace Greeley wrote about Elizabeth in his newspaper. The article drew some patients to her office.

Elizabeth's sister Emily earned her medical degree in 1854. The sisters and another doctor opened a hospital three years later. Its purpose was treating poor women and children. Emily was the surgeon. The hospital was immediately successful. The doctors needed more space to help everyone!

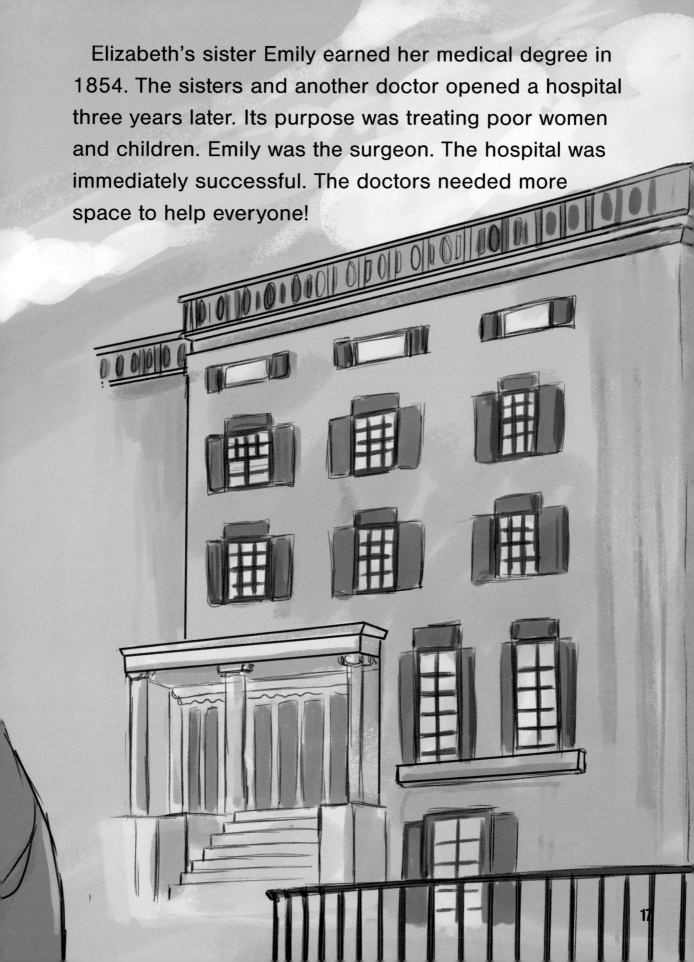

MAKING A DIFFERENCE

The Civil War began in 1861. People who wanted slavery fought those who hated it. Elizabeth and Emily supported the battle against slavery. They trained women to be nurses for **wounded** soldiers. The war ended in 1865.

Most medical schools and hospitals were still closed to women. Elizabeth decided to start a school within the hospital. Doctors could practice and improve their skills while gaining experience. Many people gave money for the project. The Women's Medical College opened in 1868.

Elizabeth missed England. She returned there in 1869. Emily ran the hospital and the school.

Elizabeth opened a medical office in London in 1869. She gave talks about health. In 1874, she helped found the London School of Medicine for Women. She wrote a book about her life in 1895.

Elizabeth died on May 31, 1910. She was 89 years old. Many women became doctors because of her **courage**. She showed how one person could change the world.

"It is not easy to be a pioneer—but oh, it is fascinating! I would not trade one moment, even the worst moment, for all the riches in the world," Elizabeth said.

TIME LINE

1821: Elizabeth Blackwell is born on February 3 in Bristol, England.

1832: The Blackwells move to the United States.

1838: Elizabeth becomes a teacher.

1847: Elizabeth enters Geneva Medical College.

1849: Elizabeth is the first woman to earn a medical degree in the U.S.

1850: Elizabeth moves to London, England.

1851: Elizabeth returns to New York City.

1857: Elizabeth opens a hospital for women and children in New York City.

1861: Elizabeth trains women to be nurses during the Civil War.

1865: The Civil War ends.

1868: Elizabeth starts a medical school for women.

1869: Elizabeth returns to England and opens a medical practice.

1874: Elizabeth cofounds the London School of Medicine for Women.

1895: Elizabeth writes a book about her life.

1910: Elizabeth Blackwell dies on May 31 in Hastings, England.

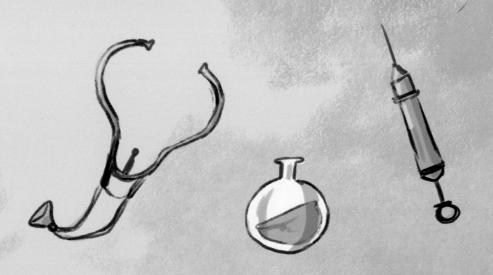

GLOSSARY

cleanliness (KLEN-lee-nis): cleanness, especially of the body and the places where people live

courage (KUR-ij): bravery; the ability to do something that scares you

equally (EE-kwuh-lee): the same for each member of a group

practice (PRAK-tis): a doctor's office

recovered (ri-KUHV-urd): got better after a difficulty

society (suh-SYE-i-tee): all people who live in the same country or region and share the same culture

surgeon (SUR-juhn): a doctor who specializes in performing operations

wounded (WOON-ded): hurt or injured

INDEX

TEXT-DEPENDENT QUESTIONS

1. What must doctors have to practice medicine?

2. When did Elizabeth Blackwell receive her medical degree?

3. Where did Elizabeth meet Florence Nightingale?

4. What happened that made Elizabeth unable to become a surgeon?

5. Why were people angry when Elizabeth opened her New York office?

EXTENSION ACTIVITY

Interview your doctor or another doctor you know. What steps did they take to become a doctor? What difficulties did they face? What advice do they have for you about pursuing a career that interests you? Write a summary of what you learned from the interview.

ABOUT THE AUTHOR

Elaine A. Kule has written fiction and nonfiction for children. She also taught reading and writing to elementary students. Elaine is glad Elizabeth Blackwell led the way for women in medicine. One such doctor solved a problem that helped the author walk again.

ABOUT THE ILLUSTRATOR

Elena Bia was born in a little town in northern Italy, near the Alps. In her free time, she puts her heart into personal comics. She also loves walking on the beach and walking through the woods. For her, flowers are the most beautiful form of life.

www.rourkebooks.com

Quote sources:
The Excellent Doctor Blackwell: The Life of the First Woman Physician, The History Press, 2006.; The Centre for Women and Democracy, "In Our Own Words: a Dictionary of Women's Political Quotations, Elizabeth Blackwell." www.cfwd.org.uk/quotatons-2/elizabeth-blackwell; Susan B. Anthony, Harriot Stanton Blatch, Matilda Gage, Ida H. Harper, Elizabeth Cady Stanton, The Complete History of Women's Suffrage, Volume I, Chapter V (Musaicum Books, 2017), 54.

Edited by: Kim Thompson
Cover and interior design by: Rhea Magaro-Wallace

Library of Congress PCN Data

Elizabeth Blackwell / Elaine A. Kule
(Women in Science and Technology)
ISBN 978-1-73161-432-2 (hard cover)
ISBN 978-1-73161-227-4 (soft cover)
ISBN 978-1-73161-537-4 (e-Book)
ISBN 978-1-73161-642-5 (ePub)
Library of Congress Control Number: 2019932138

Rourke Educational Media
Printed in the United States of America
02-1062411937